The Fabulous Cliffords

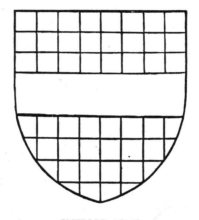

CLIFFORD ARMS.

(Checky, or and azure, a fess gules.)

A CLIFFORD WYVERN.

(Half dragon, half sea serpent.)

The Fabulous Cliffords

W R MITCHELL

CASTLEBERG
2002

For

EDWARD O'BRIEN

Who enthused about the author's story of the Cliffords – and checked it for accuracy.

A **Castleberg** Book

First published in the United Kingdom in 2002

Copyright © W R Mitchell 2002

The moral right of the author has been asserted

ISBN 1 871064 48 1

Typeset in Giovanni, printed and bound in the
United Kingdom by Lamberts Printers,
Station Road, Settle, North Yorkshire, BD24 9AA

Published by Castleberg, 18 Yealand Avenue, Giggleswick,
Settle, North Yorkshire, BD24 0AY

Contents

THIS SKIPTON CASTLE WAS REPAYRED BY THE LADY
ANN CLIFFORD, COVNTESSE DOWAGER OF
PEMBROOKEE, DORSETT, AND MONTGOMERY,
BARONESSE CLIFFORD, WEST MERLAND, AND
VESEIE, LADY OF THE HONOR OF SKIPTON IN
CRAVEN, AND HIGH SHERIFF ESSE BT INHERITANCE
OF THE COVNTIE OF WESTMORLAND, IN THE
YEARES 1657 AND 1658, AFTER THIS MAINE PART OF
ITT HAD LAYNE RVINOVS EVER SINCE DECEMBER
1648, AND THE JANVARY FOLLOWINGE, WHEN ITT
WAS THEN PVLLD DOWNE AND DEMOLISHT,
ALLMOST TO THE FOVNDACON, BY THE COMMAND
OF THE PARLIAMENT, THEN SITTINGE AT
WESTMINSTER, BECAVSE ITT HAD BIN A GARRISON
IN THE THEN CIVILL WARRES IN ENGLAND. ISA.
CHAP. 58, VER. 12. GODS NAME BE PRAISED.

FOREWORD
by Ian Lockwood
(Editor of the *Craven Herald & Pioneer*)

I'm just about old enough to remember Bill Mitchell's original series of articles in the Craven Herald. With their distinctive "milled" rule border, they stood out in the paper sent to my parents' home back in the Sixties. For a youngster, the tales of dashing adventures and medieval barbarity (see Murder Most Foul, chapter 6) formed the most exciting bit of the paper.

Wind the clock forward almost four decades and I'm delighted that Bill has finally decided to update and reprint the originals because the Cliffords of Skipton Castle have a fascinating tale to tell. They were around at the time of, and indeed playing a significant role in, some of the most momentous occasions in English history – Bannockburn, The Hundred Years War, The Wars of the Roses, The Spanish Armada, The Civil War.

For people of Skipton, the Cliffords' service for King, Queen and country ensured that the town achieved the importance it has today. Looking down on Skipton from their lofty castle perch on the rock above Eller Beck they shaped the early history of the town. Without them Skipton might have remained simply a small, unimportant village. Their most obvious legacy is the castle, which is rightly described as one of the best preserved in the North of England and in the 21st century it draws thousands of visitors each year. While the Cliffords' castle provided succour and sustenance to the townsfolk in medieval times, today it continues to provide income and benefit for the town. We have much to thank them for.

Our Illustrations

Front cover – Lady Anne Clifford when young.
George Clifford, her father, in all his splendour.
Back cover – Skipton Castle gateway seen from behind,
showing the Clifford motto – Des or Mais.
The help of Skipton Castle in the selection of these pictures and
that of Francis Clifford is warmly acknowledged. The study of
the Castle on page 43 is from the archives of Skipton Reference
Library. Uncredited photographs by the author.

One

VETERAN OF THE MARCHES

In March, 1310, Robert de Clifford – a dark, grim-faced veteran of the Welsh and Scottish Marches – was granted for life the Castle and Honour of Skipton. Robert, then in his mid-thirties, took time off from the interminable warfare with the Scots to establish his family in an area set well back from the troubled borderland. The grant, which included the Forest of Barden and the lordships of Silsden, Stirton and Thorlby, was confirmed in the following year. Robert and his heirs might retain it in perpetuity, in exchange for military service and certain lands of his inheritance in Monmouthshire. A penny, to be paid every Michaelmas, secured him a house in a part of London that became known as Clifford's Inn.

Robert had been offered land in Scotland. Reasoning that what was easily gained might just as easily be lost, he switched to Westmorland – the land west of the moors – thence to Skipton, or sheep-town, moving his family into a castle built on rock by Robert de Romille. Here the Cliffords had security and a vantage-point for traffic using the Aire Gap, an easy line of communication through the north-south barrier of the Pennines.

Robert de Clifford's ancestors, whose surname was Pons, had arrived in England with the Conqueror. A fortunate marriage brought into their possession Clifford Castle, near Hay, in Herefordshire. They took their surname from that grim fortress on the Welsh Marches and, ever looking to the future, selected Desormais or Henceforth as their motto. This first Clifford lord of Skipton married Maud de Clare, whose family had strong Irish connections, lending their name to what became known as County Clare. The descendants of Robert and Maud Clifford were to dominate the life of Skipton, of Craven and of a large part of Westmorland for almost four centuries. At first violent and martial, the House of Clifford had, by the end of the fifteenth century, lost its lust for war.

Robert, like many another Norman lord with a dash of Norse blood in his veins, was ill-mannered, lacking social graces. The first nine lords of Skipton would die violently. Yet the Clifford lords of Skipton would marry well and, despite a high infant mortality, maintain a male line; they would become Barons at the end of the thirteenth century and Earls in the sixteenth. Their early loyalty to the Crown is evidenced by a story concerning Walter de Clifford, Baron of the Marches in the twelfth century who, despite handling an officer badly, forcing the luckless man to eat the King's Writ, wax and all, regained the favour of the monarch.

Robert de Clifford, who was born about 1273, lived through the worst days of the troubles between Normanised England and her more primitive neighbours to the west and north. When campaigning, he rode a powerful war-horse of the type that was being imported from the Continent at the immense cost of around £30. He was so weighed down by armour the old command of "charge" was undertaken at a ponderous trot!

Robert was present when Edward I – the "Hammer of the Scots" – died on the bleak Solway marshes, his eyes turned to the blue hills of Scotland. In 1297, Robert de Clifford entered Annandale from Carlisle and, with his men, slew over three hundred Scots.

Robert Bruce was subsequently proclaimed King of Scotland and began to whip up unity and keen nationalism. Robert and the Earl of Pembroke defeated the Bruce's forces at St John's Town.

The Clifford fortunes in the north had been on the upturn from 1269, when Robert's father, Roger, married Isabella, daughter and co-heiress of Robert de Veteripont (or Vipont), giving the family a sizeable stake in Westmorland. This included much of the fan-shaped Eden Valley and, in particular, Brougham Castle, a bulwark against Scottish raiders. When Isabella's sister, Idonea died, having married twice but failed to produce a child, all the Veteripont possessions were absorbed into the Clifford estates.

Two

THE CLIFFORDS ARRIVE

Skipton – the Sciptone of the Domesday Book – had formed part of the domain of Earl Edwin, a Saxon whose main seat was at Bolton, in the valley of the Wharfe. In the days of the Romilles, black-robed Augustinian canons, originally allocated land at breezy Embsay, were enabled to move to a sheltered spot at Bolton. Here they praised God and built up an estate with about 2,000 sheep, each worth a shilling, the wool being valued at half a crown a stone. Robert admired the monks of Bolton because of their rock-hard faith and good works. Especially did he admire Prior de Land, who had constructed the Prior's lodging and chapel.

Robert and Maude had two sons and a daughter. Roger, the elder son, joined his father in hunting trips into the wildwood, including Sharphaw and Crookrise, the resorts of deer and wild boar. Robert devoted most of his time to campaigning against the

Scots but also replaced a stark castle at Skipton, introducing round towers, of a type familiar to Crusaders. His deer park was not for show. Deer provided fresh meat in winter when the majority of people lived off dry, salted meat – or whatever they could catch.

A man of action, he died violently at Bannockburn in 1314 when, though the Scots were outnumbered three to one, the English came off second best. The body of Robert de Clifford was sent to Edward II, who had moved to Berwick. Robert's last resting-place was possibly at his beloved Bolton Priory. Bannockburn threw England on to the defensive for some fifteen years. The Scots ran riot in northern England, gaining access to the rich lands of Craven through Edenvale.

THREE

TREASONABLE

Roger de Clifford was fourteen years old when his father was slain in battle. Mistakingly linking himself with other barons against the King, he joined an army led by Thomas, Earl of Lancaster. At the Battle of Boroughbridge, the barons were defeated and Roger, gravely injured, was taken prisoner. A military court, meeting at Pontefract, did not pursue the charge against him in view of the serious injuries he had received. The King seized the Clifford lands. Roger, a bachelor, though with some "natural" children by his mistress, died in 1327. Roger's younger brother, another Robert, became 3rd Lord and had those lands restored to him through a general act of restitution in the reign of Edward III. He was a "carpet knight," preferring a leisurely life in courtly circles to that of draughty north-country castles.

Robert married Isabel, daughter of Maurice, 2nd Lord Berkeley and they had three sons and a daughter. At the age of 28 years, Robert quit London to be host to the Scottish king in a memorable stag hunt that took place in Whinfell Forest, near Penrith. Roger became Warden of the West Marches. He died, aged thirty-eight, in May, 1344.

The violent Clifford strain that began on the Welsh Marches had by no means worked itself out. Another Robert, 4th Lord, not yet 16 when his father died, took the Clifford coat-of-arms to France, at the start of the Hundred Years War. He died while campaigning, a few months before an English victory at Crecy. Little can be written of the 4th Lord. Like a bright comet, he flashed across the sky – and was gone. Robert had married Euphemia, daughter of Ralph, Lord Neville, of Middleham in Wensleydale; there were no children and after her husband's death she lived long enough to re-marry – twice. Euphemia died in 1393.

Robert's brother, Roger, assumed the title. The 5th Lord was spirited and also wise and prudent. Like most of his forebears, his energy was dissipated through skirmishes with the Scots. He served as Warden of the Western Marches and, joining an expedition of Richard II into Scotland, had a retinue of sixty men at arms and forty archers. During a lull in fighting the Scots, Roger married Maud, daughter of Thomas Beauchamp, 3rd Earl of Warwick, and they had two sons and three daughters. When Roger enlarged his castle of Brougham, he proudly displayed a stone carving on which the arms of Clifford impaled those of Beauchamp. Having a pool and a canal excavated to connect the rivers Lowther and Eamont, he named the pool after Maud.

Roger Clifford went to sea. In May, 1388, he was with the Admiral of the Fleet on a highly successful naval expedition against the combined fleets of France and Castile. He lived to be 56 years of age and, unusually for a Clifford, he died in bed. His last resting-place was probably at Shap, the only abbey in Westmorland.

Four

THE WILD ONE

Thomas, 6th Lord of Skipton, born in 1363, became a close friend of Richard II, who was noted for his loose living. For a time, Thomas emulated him. Two years before he succeeded his father, as Lord of Skipton, Parliament charged him with aiding the king in his dissolute conduct. He eventually fell in with the spirit of the age – a relaxed, chivalrous age, a peaceful interlude in relations with France and Scotland.

As Sir Thomas Clifford, he was made Governor of Carlisle for life and became a close attendant on Richard II, who referred to him as "our very dear and loyal knight." His fondness for jousting prompted him to cross the Channel and accept a challenge from a French knight. Thomas died in 1391 while on a Crusade with the Teutonic Knights "in parts beyond the seas" (East Prussia). His widow, Elizabeth Lady Clifford, held the office of Sheriff of Westmorland until the coming of age of John, the 7th Lord, who was but three years old. When Elizabeth died in 1424, the parish church had been burnt down and so she was interred in Bondgate Church.

In 1404, aged fifteen, John married Elizabeth Percy, daughter of the renowned Harry Hotspur. He was summoned to Parliament as a baron and attended the coronation of Henry V. In 1415, having gone to France with the King, he fought in the battle of Agincourt. On his return to England, he served the King in northern parts, having the support of six hundred trusty soldiers – two hundred men-at-arms and four hundred archers.

John was the second member of his family to become a Knight of the Order of the Garter. After useful service, he fell during the siege of Meaux in 1422, aged thirty-three. His bones were brought back to Bolton and interred in the north aisle of the Priory. An inset on the blue marble tombstone was for part of the insignia he received at the Garter ceremony. The campaigning soldier was to be remembered at Appleby as the builder of a magnificent castle gatehouse. Carved on the archway, the arms of Veteriponts and Percies joined those of the Cliffords.

FIVE

SLAIN AT ST ALBANS

Thomas, the 8th Lord, was seven years old when his father died in France. In his day, Skipton Castle was not in continual occupation, the family having moved to one or other of their Westmorland castles. John was engaged in an old Clifford occupation – keeping the Scots at bay. He visited Skipton but twice in the year 1437 – firstly when en route for Conisborough and secondly, in August, when Thomas and his wife were here long enough for their horses to crop the grass in the Old Park.

Joan was the daughter of Thomas, 7th Lord Dacre, whose family had agreed to a marriage portion of 1,100 marks. The couple had four sons and six daughters. Thomas rebuilt a large part of Appleby Castle, and an adjacent chapel. The number of lodges in Barden Forest was increased from six to eight, ensuring adequate supervision and protection for the deer and other game animals.

England's long and disastrous war against France dragged to its close. Thomas fought loyally and imaginatively. When Pontoyse, near Paris, was under siege in 1437, and snow fell, he arrayed himself and his men in white so they might approach the grim fortress unobserved.

There followed a dynastic conflict, popularly known as the Wars of the Roses. It began with the Battle of St Albans in May, 1455, and ended, thirty years later, with the triumph of Henry VII at Bosworth. The remaining members of the English nobility formed groups so powerful they were able to maintain their own armies. Eventually, two main factions were involved – Lancaster (the King's party) and York. The Cliffords supported the Lancastrian cause.

Thomas, aged forty, died at St Albans. The outnumbered Lancaster force had a serious reversal. The King was taken captive and among the slain were Thomas, who was commanding the vanguard, his uncle the Earl of Northumberland and the Duke of Somerset. Their bodies were left naked in the street. John, his twenty-year-old son, found what remained of Thomas. He and his illustrious friends, were interred in the grounds of the nearby monastery.

Six

MURDER MOST FOUL

Shrovetide, 1458. John – son of Thomas – attend-ed a council with other lords whose fathers had perished at St Albans. Arrangements were made for prayers to be said for their souls. It was affirmed that the Yorkists owed them compensation. This did not trouble them for the campaign was going well. They had twice captured the King. In December, 1460, John's life – and the fortunes of the Clifford family – were transformed by a killing frenzy at the Battle of Wakefield. John, the main commander, fought so well he was knighted on the battlefield but – with vengeance against the killers of his father in mind – he was said to have decapitated the Duke of York's corpse, placing on the head a paper crown. The Duke's head and those of the young Earl of Rutland and Richard Neville, Earl of Salisbury were set over the gates of York.

It was further implied that when, by chance,

Clifford came across Edmund, the Earl of Rutland, young son of the Duke of York, and the boy knelt and asked for mercy, he drew his dagger and held it before the face of his captive, remarking: "Thy father killed my father; therefore die!" He pushed the blade into the lad's heart and was subsequently nicknamed Butcher or Black-faced Clifford.

(His acts of bitter cruelty on the battlefield are not to be doubted. Yet the tale of how he treated the young Earl Edmond is unlikely. It was recounted by Shakespeare, who used the story to illustrate vengeance working its way through three generations of the House of Clifford. Slaying the children of one's enemies was not a custom of the time. In the volatile conditions of that period, the situation might be reversed. Edmund, who was seventeen at the time, probably fell in battle).

Butcher Clifford had but three months to live. On the day before Lancaster and York clashed at Towton, he was with his troops near Castleford when a headless arrow struck him in the throat. He died immediately. What happened to his body remains a mystery. It may have been dumped in a pit dug out for others slain at Towton. Or, as he died some time before the conflict, there could have been time to move his body to the Cliffords' spiritual home at Bolton Priory, by the Wharfe. In the year of his death, the Cliffords were stripped of their honours and estates. The Stanley family and, later, Richard Duke of Gloucester, assumed the Lordship of Skipton. The Clifford family had sunk to its nadir.

Attention now switched to John's sons. His widow, Margaret, was the only daughter of Sir Henry Blomflete, of Londesborough, in East Yorkshire. Through John's marriage to her, the Cliffords had acquired the title of Vescy. Margaret ensured her sons had safe quarters – Richard on the Continent (where he died) and the other, Henry, to her family's East Yorkshire estate, where he was reared by a local couple. The man was a shepherd. His wife had been a nursery-maid at Skipton Castle.

The Yorkists, after their resounding victory at the Battle of Towton, questioned Margaret concerning the whereabouts of her two sons. She asserted that both had gone to the Continent for safety.

(The Clifford strain survived in isolation but in Yorkshire rather than on the bleak fells of Cumberland. Henry's exile and rustic upbringing is the stuff of which legends are made. How did this legend take form and credibility? Hall, the chronicler, wrote in 1548, a quarter of a century after Henry's death: "Thomas Clifford [it was actually Henry] was brought up wt a sheppard in poor habit and dissimuled behaviour, ever in feare to publish his lignage of degre." Holinshead took the story from Hall and Shakespeare read it in a work by Holinshead. The tale of the Shepherd Lord was romanticised by William Wordsworth, who doubtless liked to think that he was writing about links with his native Cumbria:

> *Love had he found in huts where poor men lie;*
> *His daily teachers had been woods and rills,*
> *The silence that is in the starry sky,*
> *The sleep that is among the lonely hills…).*

In her lifetime, Margaret saw the attainder against the Cliffords reversed and her son, Henry, proclaimed 10th Lord. She died in 1493 and was buried at Londesborough. An inscription on her tomb described her as the late wife of the most noble man John Lord Clifford. There is no mention of her second husband, Launcelot Threlkeld.

SEVEN

THE SHEPHERD LORD

In 1485 the war ended. Henry was restored "in blood and honours". Having been secretly brought up by a shepherd for seven formative years, it must have been an awesome experience to be sought out by a cavalcade of notables, keen to see his return to Skipton. Henry's re-instatement in society when he was over thirty years old was not easy. He needed help when signing his name, laboriously writing down the initial "C" of Clifford and leaving it to an attendant to fill in the rest.

He was none the less a quick learner and, keen on education, he founded a grammar school at Skipton. Preferring to live at Barden rather than Skipton, which was quieter, he developed his interest in astrology and alchemy. Henry had the forest keeper's lodge enlarged, at the same time providing a neighbouring chapel and priest's house. Forty officers and servants attended to his needs at Barden. An abstract of domestic expenses for 1510 revealed that saint days were occasions for feasting and jollity. He paid for strings for a fiddle, a bagpipe, a livery jacket for young Long the Piper, the services of minstrels, for drums and shawmes, and for players from Halifax on St Thomas's Day. A tun of wine was transported from York, a swan from Appleby and salt fish from Hartlepool.

Henry enjoyed periodic visits to London. In 1494, when there was a great banquet in Westminster Hall, he was one of four noblemen who waited on the King. Henry and Lord Harrington were installed in the "queen's closet," as opposed to the Parliament chamber where commoners had their beds and baths, and wore hermits' gowns while keeping vigil all night in the chapel. On the following morning, after hearing mass, they changed into their richest clothes and processed into the presence of the King to be dubbed knights. At a protracted feast that followed, Henry Clifford "sat among the ladies."

He was married twice and had three sons and five daughters. His first wife, Ann, was the daughter of Sir John St John, a distant cousin of the King. To her was born a son, who was given the same name as his father. When Ann died, Henry began to court Florence, a daughter of Henry Pudsay, Esquire. (Florence was a social-climber. Henry was her second husband and, on his death, she wed Richard, son of the Marquis of Dorset. He was grandson of a Queen).

BARDEN.

EIGHT

HENRY AT FLODDEN

August, 1513. Henry VIII, with the cream of his Army, was warring against the French. His brother-in-law, James IV of Scotland, had received a message from the French Queen suggesting that he might take some of the pressure from her land by staging a Second Front. James invaded England with an army of about 40,000 men and some new and impressive artillery. Henry Clifford, now sixty years old, hurriedly mustered the brawny lads of Craven and took them off to support troops under the command of the Earl of Surrey, who had been charged with the defence of the border and, at the age of seventy, was plagued with rheumatism. A metrical history caught the spirit of the times:

> *From Penigent to Pendle-hill,*
> *From Linton to Long Addingham,*
> *And all that Craven coasts did till*
> *They with the lusty Clifford came.*

All Staincliffe hundred went with him,
With striplings strong from Whorledale,
And all that Hauton-hills did climb,
With Longstroth eke and Litton Dale.
Whose milk-fed fellows freshly bred,
Well brown'd, with sounding bows upbend,
All such as Horton fells had fed
On Clifford's banners did attend.

The Scots advanced into Northumberland, destroying and plundering as they went. James, with the pick of Scotland's warriors, had the numerical edge on the English army. He established himself on the steep brow of Flodden Edge, a move that had tactical advantages. The Earl of Surrey approached with 26,000 hastily-recruited men who lacked cohesion.

On 9 September, 1513, was fought a battle that subdued the Scots for many years. Clifford, in command of the centre of the English van, conveyed a message to the Scottish host inquiring about the rules of battle. Warfare, though bloody, was chivalrous, especially when James IV was associated with it. The Scots sought to demoralise the English by declaring that no quarter would be given. The armies locked in fearful hand-to-hand conflict in which the English halberd proved itself handier than the 12 ft pikes carried by the Scotsmen. Before evening, King James and the flower of Scottish nobility had been slain. James died when a stroke from a halberd shattered his head. The Craven contingent captured and retained some of the Scottish artillery, installing "three of the seven systers" at Skipton Castle.

Not all the brave men who had followed Henry Clifford returned. Ann, of Kildwick, lost her lover in the battle.

> *Thus did she mourn and wander in the vale*
> *Till echo learnt her melancholy tale.*

NINE

THE FIRST EARL

The ten years between Flodden and the death of Henry Clifford were far from peaceful. His second wife, who was much younger than he, was a jealous woman. His son and heir by his first marriage became reckless and extravagant. Young Henry spent his youth in the glittering company of the Prince of Wales – the future King Henry VIII – and climbed socially until he could scarcely climb any more. In short, the man who would become 11th Lord of Skipton had a merry round of activity, involving wine, women, song and lawlessness.

For a year or two he was an outlaw, heading a band of men who raided religious houses and terrorised whole villages. His father mentioned some of his concerns about his son in a letter to a privy councillor. Young Henry threatened his servants, "saying that if ought came to mee he shold utterlie destroe al." He also "spoiled my houses and feloniously stole away my propre goods, w'ch was of grete substance onlie of malyce and for maynteinying his inordinate pride and ryot, as more speciallie dye apere when dep'tyd out of ye corte, and com into ye countrie, aparellyd himself and hys horse in cloth of golde and goldsmyth's wark, more lyk a duke than a pore baron's sonne as hee ys."

Henry, Shepherd Lord, expired in 1523, aged seventy. No head of the House of Clifford had lived for so long. Few had died, as he did – tucked up in bed. He directed that if he was to die in Brougham or Brough, he should be buried in Shap Abbey. If his death occurred at Skipton, then his mortal remains should be taken to Bolton Priory. His last resting-place is not known. It was probably in the family vault before the high altar at Bolton Priory.

Young Henry, 11th Lord of Skipton, emptied his system of the wildness and recklessness that earlier Cliffords had dissipated in fighting England's traditional enemies – the Welsh, Scots and French. He was to become the greatest of the family, socially and as a landowner. In 1525, Henry VIII bestowed on his friend the honour of 1st Earl of Cumberland and he became President over the Northern parts of England

and Lord Warden of the Marches.

Earl Henry married three times. His first bride, Margaret Talbot, daughter of the 4th Earl of Shrewsbury, was at the time of the marriage little more than a child and she died childless. Henry subsequently married Margaret Percy, daughter of Henry, Earl of Northumberland, and thereby brought into the Clifford family the Craven lands known as the Percy Fee. He might now ride from Skipton to Appleby and scarcely leave his own land. Margaret, who gave birth to two sons and four daughters, relieved the lst Earl of a recurrent Clifford worry. The line would not die out for want of a male heir.

When, in 1536, the King obtained from Parliament a Bill that gave him possession of all monastic foundations valued at less than £200 a year, Bolton Priory was among them. The lst Earl took over the Priory and its extensive lands, plus some of the land that had belonged to the dissolved Priory of Marton. Before Prior Moone and his canons surrendered to the King and local people watched sadly as the buildings by the Wharfe were partly dismantled and the bells and lead from the roof were sold and carted away, there occurred an episode that demonstrated the first Earl's devotion to the Crown. Henry was made a Knight of the Garter for his courage and loyalty in holding out for the King in the rebellion known as the Pilgrimage of Grace. Monastic lands were transferred to him at very special rates.

TEN

A CASTLE UNDER SIEGE

In the autumn of 1536, Henry, 1st Earl of Cumberland and the 11th Lord of Skipton, anxiously toured Skipton Castle, inspecting his followers and ensuring that his family home could withstand an attack from rebels in the Pilgrimage of Grace. It was written: "The earl had hard work to hold his castle of Skipton, weakened as it was by wholesale desertion, against the rebels' siege."

Robert Aske had mustered an army forty thousand strong. Earl Henry wrote to Lord D'Arcy, as representing the loyalist position, only to find that D'Arcy supported the uprising. Aske took York without opposition. Skipton remained loyal to the King. Earl Henry, invited to join the rebels, reaffirmed his loyal support. Part of the castle's defence was "great ordnance" collected as booty on Flodden Field.

Unexpectedly, Christopher and John, brothers of Robert Aske, and forty men, joined the Earl at Skipton

– a day before Henry's retinue of 500 men left to join the opposition. In the siege that followed, the castle was pronounced strong and abundantly provisioned. Henry VIII, impressed by the size of the rebel army, played for time. Meeting leaders of the rebels, he made promises he did not intend to keep and, all the time, built up strength to overcome them. Believing that their demands would be met, the rebels dispersed. When nothing happened, a second wave of protest began – to be ruthlessly crushed by the King's men. The leaders were executed.

After weeks of siege, Skipton Castle surrendered to the rebels. In a letter to the King, Earl Henry lamented that the rebels "spoiled" his house, removed his treasure and "had torne his evidences in peeces." A grateful monarch waited for a decent amount of time to elapse and then arranged for Bolton Priory and its estates to be made over to the Cliffords. What remained of the Priory was rented to the Earl for £19.13s.10d. The land was sold to him for a modest £2,490. The Priory, which had not been involved in the uprising, had met the fate meted out to the others.

Henry, 1st Earl, was delighted to acquire the

Bolton property and lands. His family had been feudal overlords and patrons of the Priory since early in the fourteenth century. Henry, who died in 1542, would be remembered for enlarging Skipton Castle to accommodate his newly-married son and his bride, who was Eleanor Brandon, the King's niece.

Margaret, the Earl's widow, lived into old age and found pleasure in hunting deer with greyhounds.

PENDRAGON CASTLE.

(As it was in 1739).

ELEVEN

AN AMIABLE MAN

Skipton Parish Church, 1542. For the first time, a Clifford was being laid to rest here. Bolton Priory, the burial place of earlier generations, was now a shambles. A vault had been cut below the altar in Holy Trinity Church to receive the lead coffin containing the body of Henry, 1st Earl of Cumberland. Priests intoned. The little town was hushed, except for dark horses that whinneyed and impatiently pawed the ground outside.

Standing with the widow, Margaret Percy, was her son Henry, a tall, slender man with a long nose who, aged twenty-five, had become the 2nd Earl of Cumberland and 12th Lord of Skipton. Beside him was Lady Eleanor, his wife, a woman of heavy build but regal bearing. They had been married for six years, the ceremony taking place at Brandon House, Bridewell. Chief among the guests, bluff and smiling, was King Henry, the bride's uncle. Earl Henry, an amiable man, lived in a relatively peaceful age – a time of new ideas, of liberalising forces and of curiosity about the natural world. Life with Lady Eleanor was pleasant but expensive. The couple were very much in love. "Dere Hart," she addressed him in a letter written when they had been parted. The letter was sent "To My Mose Lovynge Lord and Husband, the Earl of Cumberland." As the cost of living up to his social standing and aspirations rose alarmingly, he parted with an old Clifford possession in Herefordshire to meet outstanding bills. During ten years of marriage, two sons were born and died in infancy. Then Eleanor, while staying at Brougham, gave birth to a daughter, who was christened Margaret. When Eleanor died, she was laid to rest in the vault made for the Earl's father and mother.

London ceased to attract the Earl. One of the few occasions on which he travelled to the capital was to pay his respects to a new sovereign, the young Queen Elizabeth. Not long after Eleanor's death, Henry had a mysterious sickness. When his physicians pronounced him dead, he was stripped, laid out and

Continued on page 49

Skipton Castle, showing *(above)* one of the round towers and *(below)* a yew tree planted by Lady Anne in The Conduit Court.

Above: Bolton Priory, where some of the early Cliffords were interred. *Below:* Brasses on the tomb slab of Henry, the first Earl, in Skipton Parish Church.

Margaret Percy and her husband, Henry, first Earl
of Cumberland, as portrayed on their tomb in
Skipton Parish Church.

Two Clifford castles: Skipton *(above)* and *(below)*
Appleby's immense keep as it was in 1739.

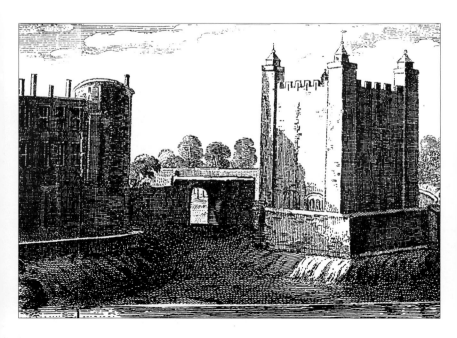

Francis Clifford, 4th Earl of Cumberland
(1559-1641).

Margaret Russell, who married George Clifford,
the parents of Lady Anne. *(Courtesy: National
Portrait Gallery)*.

Above: Nappa Hall, Wensleydale, home of the Metcalfes, who were kinsfolk of Lady Anne Clifford.
Below: Almhouses at Beamsley, near Bolton Abbey, founded by Margaret *(as portrayed on the opposite page)*.

Cliffords in Edenvale

Left: The Countess Pillar, near Brougham.

Below: Ninekirks, a church rebuilt by Lady Anne and bearing her monograph above the communion table.

covered with a cloth of black velvet. Skipton prepared to mourn the loss of its Lord. Then an attendant detected a sign of life. The Earl was carried to his bed, where he was lagged with warm clothes and given cordials to drink. He rallied, subsisted for a whole month on human milk and recovered his health.

Five months after his wife's death, Henry married Anne, daughter of William, Lord Dacre. In contrast with his first wife, she was a quiet, homely soul who bore him three children, reinforced his love for the north-country and his vast estates and persuaded him to spend freely in Westmorland. So much money was spent on Brougham Castle there was not sufficient left to restore the castle at Brough.

Nationally, fresh troubles arose. The leading characters were Queen Elizabeth and Mary Stuart. The Cliffords, as usual, were on the side of the Crown.

AWKWARD NEIGHBOURS

Land belonging to the Nortons, a staunchly Catholic family, abutted that of the Cliffords. The Nortons lived at a hall standing near the church at Rylstone. About the year 1500, Richard Norton, lord of Rylstone, had a tower constructed on a headland of rocky ground near Crookrise, in the farthest part of his lordship. A deer park was surrounded by walls and ditches. The tower was for the summertime recreation of his family, which consisted of eleven sons and eight daughters, all fervent Catholics.

Footloose deer were to be found over most of Clifford land and hunting them was a popular occupation for the family and high-born friends. Up to fifteen keepers were employed to attend to the needs of the deer and to deter poaching. A poacher called West, who lived at Grassington, was among those detained at Skipton Castle for his offence. A serious quarrel between the Cliffords and Nortons over hunting rights developed in 1541. Crookrise, part of the Forest of Skipton, owned by the Cliffords, had a common boundary in Waterford Gill with Rylstone and the lordship of Richard Norton.

Less well defined than the beck was the boundary on the moor above. Observing that many deer were harbouring on Rylstone Fell, in Norton territory, the high-handed Cliffords, considering them to be strays and trespassed in pursuit of them, to the annoyance of the Nortons. When Richard Norton questioned the Clifford right to hunt on his ground, the matter was taken before the President and Council at York. Depositions were taken. Old men who had been foresters employed by the Cliffords on Crookrise recalled that when they were young Lady Clifford often hunted and hounded deer in the lordship of Rylstone.

The Nortons had supported the abortive Pilgrimage of Grace. Now, thirty years later, they sided with Mary Queen of Scots in her claim to the English throne, then occupied by Protestant Elizabeth. Thus national events temporarily switched the attention of the two families from local deer to national events. Leading the rebellion were the Earls of

Northumberland and Westmorland, who wished to secure for Mary Queen of Scots both her liberty and the succession in her favour.

Richard Norton, by now past middle life, had been one of the 30,000 Catholic enthusiasts who followed Robert Aske from Pontefract to Doncaster behind a banner featuring the Five Wounds of Christ. His son Christopher enrolled as a knight of Mary Stuart. It was said that when she was a captive in Bolton Castle, in Wensleydale, Christopher managed to become one of the Castle guards so as to be ready to help her. (After about six months, Mary was moved to more secure accommodation further south).

The Rising was crushed. Earl Henry, though ill, helped Lord Scrope to fortify Carlisle. The Nortons faced disaster. Christopher and his uncle Thomas were executed at Tyburn. Richard Norton died as an exile in Spanish Flanders. Norton Tower was "slighted", which was the way in feudal times. Norton lands were confiscated and – with the deer – came to the Cliffords in 1605, during the reign of James I. At about this time, old folk told of a white doe belonging to the Nortons that made a weekly pilgrimage from Rylstone to Bolton Priory. It lay on a family grave in the churchyard during divine service and then returned to Rylstone. (This unlikely tale was recorded by Whitaker, in his *History of Craven*, and romanticised by Wordsworth as The White Doe of Rylstone. The member of the Norton family associated with the albino deer was called Emily, though in truth no member of the family bore this name. The Norton connection with the district ended some thirty years before the events described).

At Skipton, in 1570, the vault under the altar of the parish church was opened and Henry, 2nd Earl of Cumberland, joined his forebears. He had died at Brougham Castle, on which he lavished much care and money. (When, much later, the vault was entered and his skeleton temporarily exposed, it confirmed that he had, indeed, been a tall, slender man with a prominent nose).

George Clifford, an eleven-year-old boy, watched the solemn ceremony of committal. George, born at Brougham, became the 3rd Earl of Cumberland and 13th Lord of Skipton. On the day after his father died, and before he had been given the news, the Earl of Bedford – aware of the Clifford titles and vast estates – sought from the Queen the wardship of George, who had been promised in marriage to Margaret, his youngest daughter. Bedford ensured that George received a good education. He spent much of his time at Woburn until, aged 12, he went to Trinity College, Cambridge, where he took a degree. At Oxford, he studied mathematics and geography.

Living in the reign of Good Queen Bess, a time when the minds of many young men of noble birth turned to the sea, George Clifford became a buccaneer.

THIRTEEN

AN UNLUCKY SEA-DOG

The Atlantic, 1589. George ran a dry tongue over parched, cracked lips and stared along the deck of *Victory*, a storm-battered ship that was drifting slowly towards land, minus her masts. George, his long, lean face matted with hair that had once been trained into a trim moustache and beard, was leading an expedition that set out hopefully for the Spanish Colonies, using ships made available by Queen Elizabeth. The enterprise began well, with a quick and safe passage to the Azores, where Faial was plundered.

Clifford was seriously injured when they came off second best in a battle with a Brazilian ship. When a mystery explosion rocked the *Victory*, his main ship, he was again injured. A storm scattered and damaged the fleet, wrecking one of the ships, which – unhappily – held most of the loot from Faial. The men were so short of food and water that whenever it rained they licked the wet decks. When it was not raining, they sucked lead bullets to stimulate their saliva glands. George and some of his men survived the expedition. Soon he was planning a voyage to the Mediterranean.

George used the Clifford's northern estates as a useful source of funds for his speculative voyages – nine in all, mostly to the West Indies. George was handsome, distinguished, courageous, incurably romantic and an outstanding navigator. He made bids for glory and money at a time when Queen Elizabeth's favourites were a band of seafarers, dedicated to relieving the Spaniards of some of their New World loot. At Court, he lived well beyond his income, hoping to restore his fortunes through nautical ventures.

His first voyage, lasting a year, began in August, 1586, the destination being the South Seas. He had four ships, including the barque *Clifford*. Two of the other vessels belonged to Sir Walter Raleigh, who joined them at Plymouth. Sail was set on the 17th. Strong winds drove them back to Dartmouth, from which they again set sail on the 29th. They landed on the Canaries, then headed west to Sierra Leone. The voyage terminated on the coast of Brazil and would have been a failure if they had not intercepted a Portuguese ship with a cargo of slaves, which they sold for 400 ducats each.

Clifford fought against the Spanish Armada in 1588, commanding a Royal ship, *Elizabeth Bonaventure*. He carried news of the victory to the Queen, who was encamped at Tilbury. A grateful and much-relieved monarch promptly knighted him. She then commissioned him to sail to the South Seas on the *Golden Lion*. George fitted out the expedition at his own expense. This voyage was a failure, a storm-battered ship making an early return to England.

Fourteen

HUSBAND AND WIFE

Firmly wedded to the sea, and forever hoping that as a bold buccaneer he might recover some of the money he had squandered, George Clifford devoted little time to his family. When, in 1577, at the age of eighteen, he had married Margaret Russell – "sweet Meg" – in the presence of the Queen, a few idyllic years were spent at his castle home in Skipton. Then he went off to seek fame, fortune and fun. His daughter, Lady Anne, would recall: "He sold much land and consumed his estate in continual building of ships, voyages, horse-racing, tilting, shooting, bowling matches and all such expensive sports."

At Skipton, in 1584, a son was born and christened Francis. He died at the age of five and was laid to rest in the family vault. Robert, their second son, born in 1585, who also died young, was interred with Margaret's ancestors at Chenies. On a January day in 1590, Margaret gave birth to a daughter, who was christened Anne. George, having just arrived back in England after his ill-fated voyage to the Azores, did not attend but did write a touching letter to his wife. Neither was the father present in Holy Trinity, Skipton, in the following month when Anne was christened, though he did travel to Skipton in March. On April 2, with his wife, young son Robert (who had not long to live) and Anne (now aged nine weeks), he left for London. Anne Clifford would not set foot in Skipton Castle for many years.

George Clifford throve in the Court of Elizabeth. In 1590, he became her jousting champion. Two years later, he was made a Knight of the Garter. He was one of the peers of the realm who sat in judgement on Mary Stuart. Queen Elizabeth enjoyed George's company. She flattered him. He was her faithful servant who, when she dropped a glove, picked it up and had it mounted with jewels so that he might display it on his hat. Elizabeth encouraged him in his maritime ventures, though took a relatively small share in the financial risk. He was loaned various ships. His maritime adventures cost him much money – and wrecked his marriage.

One of his few successful ventures was an expedition of three ships that he financed from his own resources. They returned to England with prizes valued at £100,000, of which George's share amounted to £36,000. He had a vessel built and named it *Malice Scourge* but luck continued to elude him. Engaging a merchant ship manned by Portugese in a bitter battle he stood helplessly by as the big ship sank – with all its treasures. On the largest and grandest of his expeditions, he plundered Dominica, in the West Indies and, after stiff fighting, captured Puerto Rico. By this time, his forces were so reduced by warfare and disease he had to evacuate the area.

When, in the year 1600, Queen Elizabeth granted a charter to the East India Company, George became a founder-governor and a year later his wife, Margaret, put money into the company's first voyage. He still hoped that the Queen would compensate him amply for his expenditure on her behalf but her response was limited. In 1603, George became Lord Warden of the West Marches and Captain of the City of Carlisle. He had reached the high point of his career but he and his wife separated. Anne, their daughter, grew up with mother; they were linked by a bond of deep affection.

In twenty years, the Clifford estates were saddled with debts and mortgages. George's approaching death saw husband, wife and daughter reconciled. He was forgiven his liaison with "a lady of Quality." Margaret received a letter from him and with it was a superscription, in his own hand: "To my dear wife, Countess of Cumberland, give this, of whom from the bottom of my heart, in the presence of God, I ask forgiveness for all the wrongs I have done her." Margaret and Anne were present when he lay on his death-bed in a Thames-side building in London. The tidal Thames washed the place. George had found salt water irresistible in life.

George died on October 30, 1605, aged forty-seven. The body was embalmed and transported to Skipton to lie in the Clifford vault. (Many years later, Lady Anne commissioned John Ellis, a local stone-cutter, to make an elaborate tomb. When Dr Whitaker, the historian of Craven examined the body in 1808 he found it was so well preserved that the face resembled that in the portraits).

George was the last male heir of the line that had begun with Robert de Clifford. He had willed the family estates not to his daughter, as she expected, but to a brother, Francis, and to a nephew named Henry. Perhaps George sensed that through them many of his debts would be cleared and life made more tolerable for his successors. His will mirrored his life. Each was strange and complex.

ANNE CLIFFORD.

FIFTEEN

THE LAST EARLS

George, the last of the Cliffords in the direct male line, drew up a will that was to have a profound effect on the life of Anne, his daughter. The will ignored the fact that deeds arranged as long ago as the reign of Edward II specified that the estates were entailed on heirs, regardless of sex. Only if the beneficiaries – his younger brother Francis and nephew Henry – died without male heirs would the estates come to Anne, who was bequeathed the modest sum of £15,000. In 1606 began the legal battle by which Lady Anne was determined to come into her own. She had a long task ahead; her father had died aged forty-seven. Francis lived to celebrate his eighty-first birthday.

Under the lordship of Francis, 4th Earl of Cumberland, the Clifford family fortunes were restored and Skipton burst out of its narrow feudal bounds as both freehold and leasehold tenancies became available. Francis, true Clifford in the support he gave to Royalty, was a friendly, gentle, easy-going man who kept a good table. At the Castle as many as thirty people might sit down with him and dine on such delicacies as wild duck, partridge and sea fish, washed down by ale, by currant wine and by French claret that cost the Earl three shillings a barrel. He loved apple tarts and up to a dozen were set on the table for a meal. It was said that one tenant held his farm by providing enough apples throughout the year for tarts needed at the table of his Lord. Other tenants, as part of their rental, delivered eggs to the Castle.

The entertainment provided at Skipton was mirrored at Brougham, where in 1617 Francis and his son Henry entertained James I, who was returning from a visit to Scotland. Masses of good food and drink were assembled. Glee singers brought from London featured in a special entertainment. Francis used a vast collection of shells that George, the 3rd Earl, had brought from the Caribbean, forming them into a grotto that featured Neptune, Zephyr and the Sun and Moon – by which the old-time navigators like George had found their way.

Francis's wife, Grisold, Lady Abergavenny, wearied by the protracted law-suits about inheritance, refused to live on Clifford lands. They had two sons and two daughters. Grisold died at Londesborough in 1613 and here she was buried. Neighbours like the Yorkes could be irritating, such as when in 1611 Sir John Yorke claimed free warren and chase at Appletreewick. A fight between the respective servants developed. The case was considered by the Star Chamber, which made no attempt to decide the entitlement but fined Sir John £200 for hunting and for making provoking speeches.

Henry, son of Francis, governed the Clifford estates for the last twenty years of his father's life. He held the courtesy title of Lord Clifford, though the barony had passed to Lady Anne, the 3rd Earl's daughter. Henry was an intelligent, well-educated man who was made a Knight of the Bath and served for two periods as Member of Parliament for Westmorland. His father, having breathed his last in the very room at Skipton Castle where he had been born in 1559, was laid to rest in the family vault at Skipton. Henry became the 5th and last Earl of Cumberland. He was to hold it for only two years. In the end, Lady Anne benefited from the tenure of the two men though she continued to think she had been robbed of her birthright.

Henry, 5th Earl of Cumberland, tall and well-made, with keenness and vigour, kept a tight hold on the Clifford estates during the last two decades of his father's life. On inheriting them, he had a no-nonsense attitude towards his servants and tenants. Henry married Lady Frances Cecil, daughter of Robert, Earl of Salisbury. His new father-in-law was Lord High Treasurer of England.

Frances bore him five children – three sons, two daughters – yet only one daughter, Elizabeth, survived. She married Richard Boyle, the Earl of Cork and, against a background of costly law suits, Henry strove to make some legal arrangement whereby he could leave the Clifford estates to her.

Sixteen

A Castle Holds Out

Henry played a notable part in the Civil War – the clash between Charles I and Parliament. When the conflict spluttered into life in 1642, Henry was Lord Lieutenant of the county of York. The King commissioned his officers in the counties to muster and arm the inhabitants against the Parliamentarians. Henry took command of the Royal forces in Yorkshire and, in a Declaration, set forward the Royal case, rallying more support. He subscribed £500 towards the King's service.

Many of those working on his estate were called to the colours; farm work was affected by the loss of labour and by the requisition of buildings, horses and wagons. At Bolton Abbey, the estate rents were not collected and when the conflict was over they were much reduced. Skipton Castle was subjected to a protracted siege. Three hundred men formed the garrison when the Parliamentarians arrived. Two valiant men

– Sir John Mallory, garrison commander, and General John Lambert – faced each other across the castle walls. Lambert was a local man, being a native of Calton in Malhamdale.

In 1643, the 5th Earl had died in York from a "burning fever". He was fifty years of age. A special coach was used to move his embalmed body to Skipton. Two years later, with the siege of the Castle still in operation, the King imposed a levy on Craven for the maintenance of the garrison. The Parliamentarians tightened the cordon but the garrison was not overrun. For the first two years, the besiegers were content simply to keep the garrison quiet. The siege was not absolute. There would be surreptitious comings and goings to keep the garrison provisioned. An offensive sortie took some of Mallory's men as far as Keighley. Lambert, now on a roving commission, cut them off and defeated them. One by one the Royalist strongholds of Yorkshire fell until only Skipton remained. It was never taken. The garrison surrendered on honourable terms, the defenders being settled at Newark, Oxford and Hereford.

With the death of Henry Clifford's wife shortly

after he was taken to his eternal rest in the family vault in Skipton Parish Church, Lady Anne Clifford was free to take over the Craven and Westmorland estates. A bitter family feud had been resolved by the deaths of all the male claimants. Anne, who in the meantime had become Duchess of Dorset and Countess of Pembroke, was now fifty-four years of age. Her Castle at Skipton was under the control of Henry Currer, as governor, and the garrison was formed of Roundheads.

What happened to the Clifford estates when Lady Anne travelled North was the last and, in many ways, the most splendid phase of all, spread over thirty-two years.

Seventeen

Lady Anne

The woman who left Skipton as a nine-year-old child, in the company of her parents and brother, returned in 1605 in what turned out to be her prime. Despite frequent illnesses, two marriages and excessive child-bearing, Lady Anne Clifford had kept her good looks. In her younger days, she had been small and dainty, with black eyes, quick and lively, and brown hair that, when combed out, reached to the calves of her legs.

With good tutors, titled relatives and a devoted and devout mother, she was familiar with the Court of Queen Elizabeth, her introduction coming when she was thirteen through the influence of an aunt, Anne Countess of Warwick. Anne was much loved by the Queen. Anne's mother was among the ladies of the court in attendance as the body of "that Renowned Queen" was transported by barge down the Thames from Richmond, to be carried ashore at

Whitehall. Lady Anne attended the funeral service at Westminster Abbey.

Anne became familiar with the lively, elaborate rounds of the Court of King James and Queen Anne as one of the Queen's ladies-in-waiting. The year 1605 was momentous. She and her mother were in attendance when her father died "penitently, willingly and Christianly", as Anne confided in her diary. Mother and daughter determined to continue to fight the terms of father's will. Documentary evidence was needed. In July, 1607, they went north to Appleby and, in the Castle, searched for papers that could reinforce their opinion that a wrong had been committed.

The next stop was at Brougham Castle, on the lands of Margaret's jointure. They spent three or four days in a venerable building that was rich with Clifford associations. Lady Anne was seeing it for the first time. When they headed southwards, Francis, 4th Earl, refused to admit them to Skipton Castle so they called at Beamsley, in Wharfedale, where Margaret had put the construction of almshouses in hand. A Mr Clapham gave them overnight hospitality. Back in London, the next phase of the legal battle began.

In 1609, Anne married Richard Sackville, then Lord Buckhurst – a handsome, dashing nobleman who was well connected at Court through his family and a friendship with Prince Henry. The family seat was Knole, near Sevenoaks. Like the Cliffords, the family had Royal connections. Richard enjoyed masques and tilting. He was also a scholar, having been to Oxford. Two days after the wedding, which took place at Margaret's London home, Richard's father died. The young couple became Lord and Lady Dorset. Stormy arguments ensued over Anne's attempts to regain her estates. Her husband would like her to settle for a compromise with her uncle "in this bisness of my Lande."

When Prince Henry became Prince of Wales, the ladies of the Court were the "River Nymphs of England" in a specially written masque. Lady Anne represented the Aire – the river of her birthplace. She was to think of it many times as the law suits over her heritage quickened.

Eighteen

A Mother Lost

Anne, Lady Dorset (nee Clifford) had an especially deep love for Margaret her "most affectionate, dear and excellent" mother. After the marriage of Anne to Richard Sackville, Margaret made her home at Brougham, returning to the South for the birth, in 1614, of Anne's first child, which was named Margaret. Another time, Anne met her mother at Brougham, discussing the pressure being put on her by King, husband and others to reach a settlement over the Clifford estates. The exasperated Richard wrote to her that concern for those estates "transports you beyond yourself and makes you devoid of all reason." Clifford money would enable him to sustain a life devoted to pleasure, in London or overseas.

Anne remained in the country "like an owl in a desert". Then word reached her that her mother was ill. Mother's condition deteriorated. She rallied – but died from a tumour. Anne was left alone in the fight for her inheritance. When her husband died in 1624, aged thirty-five, having accrued debts of £60,000, Anne was left with two daughters, Margaret and Isabella. Three other children, including the son for whom she had craved, had died as infants. Anne was not present at her husband's last moments. She was at the bedside of their daughter, Margaret, who was sickening for smallpox. Anne also contracted the disease.

After six years of widowhood, fashionable London was startled to learn that this titled woman, who was not yet forty years of age and was considered to be in the prime of life, had married again. The surprise came from her choice of husband, Philip Herbert, Earl of Pembroke and Montgomery – a nobleman in name only – handsome, violent, cruel, contemptible, with few friends. His main passions for dogs and horses. Philip's first wife had borne him seven sons and three daughters and two sons and a daughter survived. Anne bore him two children, who were born prematurely and died in infancy.

An argument broke out between husband and wife when he wanted Lady Isabella, Anne's daughter by her first marriage, to wed one of his sons. With the outbreak of the Civil War, Anne and Isabella, who were Royalists, went into hiding for over six years. Her husband supported Parliament. Isabella married the Earl of Northampton in 1647. Anne's marriage to Philip lasted for twenty years. In 1650, he died of "a pestilential fever". They had not lived together in later years. She was staying in Appleby, for with the death of Henry, 5th Earl of Cumberland, she had come into her own. The Clifford estates were hers "without Question or Controversie".

She spent five years putting in order her affairs in the South. No loose-ends must remain. Henry Currer, who for a time had been in charge of the garrison of Skipton Castle when it was under siege, was appointed steward of her Craven estates. He, poor chap, had been forced to preside over the slighting of the Castle by breaching its defences and selling off its armaments. Over forty tons of lead from the stripped roofs and a considerable amount of timber were sold for £450 to the Watsons of Silsden Moor. She could get even with them. They were her tenants.

On July 11, 1649, Anne took leave of her two daughters, their lords and her grandchildren and left London "onwardes on my Journey towards Skipton." Never again would she leave her northern estates.

Arriving in Skipton shortly after the Castle had been slighted, she was disposed to travel on to the somewhat dilapidated Barden Tower for accommodation.

At the side of the road, about a quarter of a mile south of Brougham Castle, she had a commemorative pillar erected. This marked the spot where, in 1616, she had last parted from her "good and pious mother". Characteristically, she left an annuity of four pounds for the poor of the parish, the money to be distributed every year on April 2, the actual day of the parting. Anne found her properties and the local churches in such a sad condition she was to spend the rest of her life – and a considerable sum of money – on their restoration. She was sixty years of age and for a time was grievously short of funds. She impressed most of those who met her by her vigour.

NINETEEN

HER LADYSHIP AT HOME

A s she was driven up to her Castle at Skipton on a
July day in 1649, Lady Anne Clifford was sad-
dened by the signs of destruction. The buildings were
decayed and smelling. Rubble from the slighted walls
lay everywhere. The Church was badly damaged.
Among the rubble was the tomb of her ancestors.
Lady Anne toured her northern estates, inspecting the
properties, returning to Skipton in February, 1650.

Anne had to cope with a cash shortage for many
tenants had not paid their rent for years and they had
become unruly. In most cases, compromise and
agreement settled any differences. Boundaries were
ridden. Old rights were asserted and neglected Courts
held. When Cromwell offered the help of officials of
the Protectorate in sorting out the confusion, Anne
bitingly remarked: "Does he imagine that I, who
refused to submit to King James, will submit to him?"
Cromwell's amusement over this appears to have

turned to admiration when she responded to his dictum that he would destroy any castles she would rebuild by stating that as often as he destroyed them she would rebuild them "while he leaves me a shilling in my pocket." The Protector announced: "Let her build them; she shall have no hindrance from me."

And build she did. During the next few years, the sound of masons and joiners at work roused the echoes at Skipton, Barden, Appleby, Brougham, Brough and Pendragon. She asserted her rights by having the bounds of her Westmorland estate ridden. One report had it that she herself mounted a horse in this process. Tenants were summoned to attend the various courts. The Watsons were allowed to keep the timber from Skipton Castle. Instead of insisting on its return, Anne made a harsh adjustment of their rent.

She restored Barden Tower, cheerfully ignoring the fact it was no longer hers. It had passed to the family of Henry, the 5th Earl – to Henry's daughter, who was now the Countess of Cork. When the Countess came to stay at her Bolton estate, Lady Anne blithely entertained her cousin at Skipton Castle and was invited back to Bolton Hall. How the Countess managed to retain her composure when Barden was filched from her is not recorded. Later, Anne journeyed to Appleby, via Kirkby Lonsdale, spending ten days at another place where the Civil War had made an unwelcome mark. The parish church at Appleby was in ruins. Her castles at Brougham, Brough and Pendragon were decayed.

At Skipton Castle, the reconstruction work was completed by the year 1663. The fittings included some handsome water pipes to carry rain from the roof. They were dated 1659 and bore Anne's mark. The gatehouse was restored. Above it, and between the handsome drum towers, was fixed in stone the old motto of the Cliffords – Desormais which in Norman French meant Henceforth. When restoring the Church, Anne added a tomb for her father. The mother whom she loved greatly had been interred at Appleby and beside it was built the richly-emblazoned tomb that she herself would occupy.

TWENTY

LIFE WITH LADY ANNE

For almost thirty years, Lady Anne was virtually a queen in the dale-country of Craven and Westmorland. Physically, she had become diminutive, slim and wrinkled, wearing rough black serge, "a dress not disliked by any, but imitated by none." Bishop Rainbow was impressed by her austerity and humility and by the fact that "…the Mistris of this Family was dieted more sparingly, and I believe many times more homely, and clad more coarsely and cheaply than most of the Servants in her House." She enjoyed smoking – or it may have been snuff-taking – for in 1673 she bought a pound of best Virginian tobacco, at a cost of four shillings, "for my owne taking." At Appleby, she warmed herself beside coal brought – at a shilling a load – from her own pits on Stainmore.

Like a queen, Anne was keen to preserve her rights, which is not surprising in view of the time and trouble she had spent in pursuing them. When a tenant who had to provide her with a brood-hen felt that his commitment might be overlooked – especially as no less than 1,600 brood-hens were due to her ladyship at Appleby and Skipton – she promptly spent over £400 in legal proceedings, won her case and received the brood-hen. The fowl was killed and roasted. The tenant was invited to share in the meal.

She was devoted to the Anglican Church, which she had staunchly supported right through the troubled days of the Commonwealth. Anne was a great restorer of churches and as with other buildings on which she spent money, she made sure that the fact of her benevolence and the date were cut in stone and prominently displayed. At the Church in Skipton, she arranged instead for window medallions to be installed; they carry her initials AP and the date 1655.

A chaplain was installed at each of her houses. If she could not attend church, perhaps through ill-health, services were conducted in her own quarters. Each morning, prayers and a chapter from the Bible were read to her. The massive Diary she began in 1652 was to be liberally sprinkled with Biblical texts. Anne used the Prayer Book during the

Commonwealth, when it was officially forbidden. She established almshouses at Appleby and extended those her mother founded at Beamsley, in Wharfedale. Those who were given quarters in the almshouses must regularly attend religious services. Anne loved the company of her "old ladies." A guest of hers might be persuaded to visit one of the almshouses and dine with the residents.

Anne found pleasure in the north-country, especially when her relatives – and particularly her grandson, John Tufton – stayed with her. She wrote: "I doe more and more fall in Love with the contentments and innocent Pleasures of Countrey Life."

LADY ANNE'S SIGNATURE.

TWENTY-ONE

UP HILL, DOWN DALE

Lady Anne liked to visit her five Castles and Barden Tower in turn. She would also drop in on notables like her steward, Edward Hasell of Dalemain, near Penrith. Here she slept in a canopied bed she had presented to the family for her own use. Of Restoration style, the woodwork was richly adorned with cherubs and also pineapple, a fruit introduced from Barbados as recently as 1670.

Anne made presents of "great large stock locks", some of which were inscribed AP. If she liked a portrait of herself she had commissioned, copies were made for her friends.

As she moved from one castle to another, the whole countryside was aware of it, as well they might; they were a reminder of the Royal Progresses she enjoyed in her young days. Sometimes her retinue totalled three hundred people. Apart from her servants and tenants, notable neighbours accompanied the old lady, up hill, down dale. The baggage-train held favourite items of furniture and tapestries; also her bedding. A heavy springless coach drawn by six horses was used by Anne and her attendants. At other times, the horse-litter was a favourite form of transport. When she was old and ailing, prone to "swounding fitts," she continued to move from place to place, remarking that she might as well die in her litter as in her bed.

Setting out from Skipton to visit the northern part of her estate, she liked to vary the route, going via Kirkby Lonsdale or even via Bowes and Stainmore. In 1663, her restless nature led her from Barden Tower, where she had been staying, to Skipton Castle – with a glimpse of the room in which she had been born in 1590. Anne then set off for Westmorland on a route that included stretches unknown to her and where, she wrote triumphantly in her Diary, no coach had been before. The first night was spent at Kilnsey, as a welcome guest of Mr Cuthbert Wade. Next day's journey was to the head of Wharfedale and the steep ascent of Buckden Raikes leading to a crossing of Stake Moss into Wensleydale and staying for the night with her kinsfolk the Metcalfes at Nappa Hall, near

Askrigg.

Anne spent two days with the Metcalfes before heading for her castle at Pendragon, in Mallerstang, a journey that involved the steep climb over Cotter End and the well-used but bumpy route leading to Hell Gill, on the boundary between Yorkshire and Westmorland. A steep descent brought her to Pendragon, beside the infant river Eden and with a dramatic backdrop in Wild Boar Fell.

Twenty-two

Finale

Her last journey, on a colourful autumn day in 1675, was from Appleby to Brougham. From May until October she had resided in her great Castle, which was looped by the River Eden and from the tower of which she had a splendid view of the northern Pennines, including mighty Cross Fell. At Brougham, wearily and thankfully, she sought out her own room and hardly left it for half a year.

The year 1676 was a time of restriction and of pain. Anne spent most of it in her chamber at Brougham, where she attended to the business of her estates and received a steady procession of visitors. She was very ill on March 19, lying in her bed for four days, "enduring all her pains with a most Christian fortitude, always answering those that asked her how she did with 'I thank God I am very well'." It was here, where her father had been born and where her mother died, that her thoughts might go wandering back down the years – to the Court of Elizabeth or that of King James and Queen Anne. Perhaps she mentally traced her noble family back to the beginning of the Clifford saga in 1310 when a stern warrior, Robert de Clifford, veteran of the Welsh Marches and now engaged in the tussle with the Scots, rode into Skipton to claim his new Honour and Estate. The Honour, confirmed in 1311, has legally passed to each successive owner of the Castle.

Lady Anne, the last of the Cliffords, died at about six o'clock in the evening of March 22. Her funeral took place at Appleby on April 14. Her body, in a close-fitting shroud of lead (there was no coffin as such) was placed on a rough stone bench immediately under her elaborate monument, which she had commissioned to be made in her lifetime. The coats of arms on her tomb collectively formed an early Debrett, for Anne in addition to being Countess Dowager of Pembroke, Dorset and Montgomery, daughter and heir of the 3rd Earl of Cumberland, was Baroness Clifford, Westmorland and Vescy, Lady of the Honour of Skipton-in-Craven and High Sheriffess of Westmorland. Anne compiled a will two years before she died, bequeathing to her daughter, Lady

Thanet, her only surviving child, a life interest in the whole of her estates. When, not long afterwards, Lady Thanet died, the Clifford estates were entailed to her favourite grandson, John Tufton.

Lady Anne Clifford is dead, but her spirit lives on in every part of her north-country estates. People still gather round the Countess Pillar, which she erected at the roadside near Brougham to mark the spot where she had last bid farewell to her mother. Her name is to be seen inscribed in stone on castles, halls and churches she restored. When it was decided that an electrical supply should be provided at her almshouses at Appleby, an old lady wondered if Lady Anne would mind.